50 Japanese Home Cooking Made Easy

By: Kelly Johnson

Table of Contents

- Teriyaki Chicken
- Miso Soup
- Okonomiyaki (Savory Pancake)
- Tonkatsu (Breaded Pork Cutlet)
- Gyudon (Beef Bowl)
- Tamagoyaki (Japanese Omelette)
- Onigiri (Rice Balls)
- Yakisoba (Stir-Fried Noodles)
- Katsudon (Pork Cutlet Rice Bowl)
- Nikujaga (Meat and Potato Stew)
- Gyoza (Japanese Dumplings)
- Ramen (Simple Home-Style)
- Udon Noodle Soup
- Soba Noodle Salad
- Chicken Katsu Curry
- Japanese Fried Rice (Chahan)
- Takoyaki (Octopus Balls)
- Tempura (Battered & Fried Seafood/Veggies)
- Shoyu (Soy Sauce) Ramen
- Oyakodon (Chicken and Egg Rice Bowl)
- Yaki Onigiri (Grilled Rice Balls)
- Sukiyaki (Beef Hot Pot)
- Nabe (Japanese Hot Pot)
- Omurice (Omelette Rice)
- Chawanmushi (Savory Egg Custard)
- Japanese Potato Salad
- Salmon Teriyaki
- Shabu-Shabu (Japanese Hot Pot)
- Agedashi Tofu (Fried Tofu in Dashi)
- Hiyayakko (Chilled Tofu)
- Mentaiko Pasta (Spicy Cod Roe Pasta)
- Unagi Don (Grilled Eel Rice Bowl)
- Yasai Itame (Stir-Fried Vegetables)
- Japanese Hamburg Steak
- Simmered Daikon Radish

- Corn Potage (Japanese Corn Soup)
- Karaage (Japanese Fried Chicken)
- Tsukemono (Japanese Pickles)
- Chashu Pork (Braised Pork for Ramen)
- Lotus Root Stir-Fry
- Japanese Cabbage Pancakes
- Gomaae (Sesame Spinach Salad)
- Mitarashi Dango (Sweet Soy Sauce Glazed Dumplings)
- Kinpira Gobo (Braised Burdock Root)
- Miso Glazed Eggplant
- Kimpira Renkon (Stir-Fried Lotus Root)
- Dorayaki (Sweet Red Bean Pancakes)
- Matcha Warabi Mochi
- Castella Cake (Japanese Sponge Cake)
- Daifuku Mochi (Sweet Rice Cake with Filling)

Teriyaki Chicken

Ingredients:

- 2 boneless, skinless chicken breasts (or thighs)
- ¼ cup soy sauce
- 2 tbsp honey or brown sugar
- 1 tbsp rice vinegar
- 1 tbsp mirin (optional)
- 1 tsp sesame oil
- 2 cloves garlic, minced
- 1 tsp ginger, grated
- 1 tbsp cornstarch + 2 tbsp water (for slurry)
- 1 tbsp vegetable oil (for cooking)
- 1 tbsp sesame seeds (for garnish)
- 2 green onions, sliced (for garnish)

Instructions:

1. **Prepare the Sauce:** In a small bowl, whisk together soy sauce, honey, rice vinegar, mirin, sesame oil, garlic, and ginger. Set aside.
2. **Cook the Chicken:** Heat vegetable oil in a pan over medium heat. Add chicken and cook for about 4-5 minutes per side until golden brown and fully cooked. Remove from the pan and set aside.
3. **Make the Teriyaki Sauce:** In the same pan, pour in the sauce mixture and bring to a simmer.
4. **Thicken the Sauce:** Mix cornstarch with water to create a slurry, then stir it into the sauce. Cook for 1-2 minutes until thickened.
5. **Coat the Chicken:** Return the chicken to the pan, coating it in the sauce. Let it cook for another minute.
6. **Serve:** Slice the chicken, garnish with sesame seeds and green onions, and serve over rice or steamed vegetables.

Miso Soup

Ingredients:

- 4 cups dashi (Japanese soup stock)
- 3 tbsp miso paste (white or red)
- ½ cup tofu, cubed
- 1 sheet wakame seaweed, rehydrated
- 2 green onions, sliced

Instructions:

1. Heat dashi in a pot over medium heat until warm but not boiling.
2. Dissolve miso paste in a small bowl with a bit of warm dashi, then stir it into the pot.
3. Add tofu and wakame, simmer for 1-2 minutes.
4. Remove from heat, garnish with green onions, and serve hot.

Okonomiyaki (Savory Pancake)

Ingredients:

- 1 cup flour
- ½ cup dashi or water
- 1 egg
- 2 cups cabbage, shredded
- ½ cup tempura scraps (tenkasu) (optional)
- 4 slices bacon or pork belly
- Okonomiyaki sauce
- Japanese mayonnaise
- Bonito flakes (katsuobushi)
- Aonori (dried seaweed flakes)

Instructions:

1. In a bowl, mix flour, dashi, and egg until smooth.
2. Fold in cabbage and tempura scraps.
3. Heat a non-stick pan and pour in the batter, shaping into a round pancake.
4. Lay bacon on top and cook for 3-4 minutes per side until golden brown.
5. Drizzle with okonomiyaki sauce, mayonnaise, and sprinkle with bonito flakes and aonori. Serve hot.

Tonkatsu (Breaded Pork Cutlet)

Ingredients:

- 2 pork loin chops
- Salt and pepper
- ½ cup flour
- 1 egg, beaten
- 1 cup panko breadcrumbs
- Oil for frying
- Tonkatsu sauce

Instructions:

1. Pound pork chops to even thickness, season with salt and pepper.
2. Dredge in flour, dip in egg, and coat with panko.
3. Heat oil to 350°F (175°C) and fry pork for 4-5 minutes per side until golden brown.
4. Drain on paper towels, slice, and serve with tonkatsu sauce.

Gyudon (Beef Bowl)

Ingredients:

- ½ lb thinly sliced beef (ribeye or sirloin)
- 1 small onion, sliced
- 1 cup dashi
- 3 tbsp soy sauce
- 2 tbsp mirin
- 1 tbsp sugar
- Cooked rice, for serving
- Pickled ginger (beni shoga) for garnish

Instructions:

1. Heat dashi, soy sauce, mirin, and sugar in a pan over medium heat.
2. Add onion and cook until soft.
3. Add beef and simmer until cooked through.
4. Serve over a bowl of rice, garnished with pickled ginger.

Tamagoyaki (Japanese Omelette)

Ingredients:

- 3 eggs
- 1 tbsp soy sauce
- 1 tbsp mirin
- ½ tsp sugar
- Oil for cooking

Instructions:

1. Beat eggs with soy sauce, mirin, and sugar.
2. Heat a small pan, lightly oil, and pour a thin layer of egg mixture.
3. Roll the egg to one side, add more egg, and continue rolling until fully cooked.
4. Slice and serve warm.

Onigiri (Rice Balls)

Ingredients:

- 2 cups cooked Japanese rice
- ½ tsp salt
- 1 sheet nori, cut into strips
- Filling (tuna mayo, salmon, pickled plum, etc.)

Instructions:

1. Wet hands, sprinkle with salt, and take a handful of rice.
2. Place filling in the center and shape into a triangle or ball.
3. Wrap with a strip of nori and serve.

Yakisoba (Stir-Fried Noodles)

Ingredients:

- 2 packs yakisoba noodles
- ½ lb pork or chicken, sliced
- 1 cup cabbage, shredded
- ½ cup carrot, julienned
- ½ onion, sliced
- 3 tbsp yakisoba sauce
- 1 tbsp oil
- Pickled ginger for garnish

Instructions:

1. Heat oil in a pan and cook meat until browned.
2. Add vegetables and stir-fry until softened.
3. Add noodles and yakisoba sauce, tossing to coat.
4. Serve hot, garnished with pickled ginger.

Katsudon (Pork Cutlet Rice Bowl)

Ingredients:

- 1 tonkatsu (see recipe above)
- ½ onion, sliced
- 1 cup dashi
- 2 tbsp soy sauce
- 1 tbsp mirin
- 1 egg, beaten
- Cooked rice

Instructions:

1. Heat dashi, soy sauce, and mirin in a pan, add onions, and simmer until soft.
2. Place tonkatsu on top and pour beaten egg over.
3. Cover and cook for 1-2 minutes until the egg is set.
4. Serve over rice.

Nikujaga (Meat and Potato Stew)

Ingredients:

- ½ lb thinly sliced beef or pork
- 2 potatoes, peeled and cut into chunks
- 1 carrot, sliced
- 1 onion, sliced
- 2 cups dashi
- 3 tbsp soy sauce
- 2 tbsp mirin
- 1 tbsp sugar

Instructions:

1. Heat a pan and cook meat until browned.
2. Add potatoes, carrot, and onion, stir-frying briefly.
3. Pour in dashi, soy sauce, mirin, and sugar, and simmer for 20 minutes.
4. Serve warm.

Gyoza (Japanese Dumplings)

Ingredients:

- ½ lb ground pork
- 1 cup cabbage, finely chopped
- 2 green onions, chopped
- 1 clove garlic, minced
- 1 tsp ginger, grated
- 1 tbsp soy sauce
- 1 tsp sesame oil
- Gyoza wrappers
- Oil for frying
- Water for steaming

Instructions:

1. Mix pork, cabbage, green onions, garlic, ginger, soy sauce, and sesame oil in a bowl.
2. Place a small spoonful of filling into each wrapper, fold, and seal.
3. Heat oil in a pan, place gyoza flat-side down, and cook until golden brown.
4. Add a splash of water, cover, and steam for 2-3 minutes.
5. Serve with dipping sauce.

Ramen (Simple Home-Style)

Ingredients:

- 4 cups chicken or pork broth
- 2 packs fresh or dried ramen noodles
- 2 tbsp soy sauce
- 1 tbsp miso paste (optional)
- 1 tsp sesame oil
- 1 clove garlic, minced
- ½ tsp ginger, grated
- ½ cup mushrooms, sliced
- 2 green onions, chopped
- 2 boiled eggs, halved
- Sliced nori for garnish

Instructions:

1. Heat sesame oil in a pot and sauté garlic and ginger until fragrant.
2. Add broth, soy sauce, and miso paste, and bring to a simmer.
3. Cook noodles according to package instructions, then drain.
4. Divide noodles into bowls and pour the hot broth over them.
5. Top with mushrooms, green onions, boiled eggs, and nori. Serve hot.

Udon Noodle Soup

Ingredients:

- 2 packs udon noodles
- 4 cups dashi (Japanese soup stock)
- 2 tbsp soy sauce
- 1 tbsp mirin
- ½ tsp salt
- ½ cup green onions, chopped
- ½ cup tempura flakes (optional)
- 1 soft-boiled egg (optional)

Instructions:

1. In a pot, heat dashi, soy sauce, mirin, and salt.
2. Cook udon noodles according to package instructions and drain.
3. Divide noodles into bowls and pour the broth over them.
4. Garnish with green onions, tempura flakes, and a soft-boiled egg if desired. Serve hot.

Soba Noodle Salad

Ingredients:

- 2 packs soba noodles
- 1 tbsp soy sauce
- 1 tbsp rice vinegar
- 1 tbsp sesame oil
- ½ tsp sugar
- 1 cucumber, julienned
- ½ cup shredded carrots
- 2 tbsp sesame seeds
- 1 green onion, sliced

Instructions:

1. Cook soba noodles, drain, and rinse under cold water.
2. Mix soy sauce, vinegar, sesame oil, and sugar to make the dressing.
3. Toss noodles with cucumber, carrots, and dressing.
4. Garnish with sesame seeds and green onions. Serve chilled.

Chicken Katsu Curry

Ingredients:

- 2 chicken breasts
- Salt and pepper
- ½ cup flour
- 1 egg, beaten
- 1 cup panko breadcrumbs
- Oil for frying
- 2 cups Japanese curry sauce
- 2 cups cooked rice

Instructions:

1. Season chicken with salt and pepper.
2. Dredge in flour, dip in egg, and coat with panko.
3. Fry in oil at 350°F (175°C) until golden brown and cooked through.
4. Heat curry sauce in a pan and serve over rice.
5. Slice katsu and place on top of the curry.

Japanese Fried Rice (Chahan)

Ingredients:

- 2 cups cooked rice (day-old is best)
- ½ cup cooked shrimp or diced chicken
- ½ cup green onions, chopped
- ½ cup mixed vegetables (peas, carrots, corn)
- 1 egg, beaten
- 1 tbsp soy sauce
- 1 tbsp sesame oil
- ½ tsp salt

Instructions:

1. Heat sesame oil in a pan and scramble the egg. Remove and set aside.
2. Add shrimp/chicken, vegetables, and green onions, stir-frying for 2 minutes.
3. Add rice and mix well, then stir in soy sauce and salt.
4. Return scrambled egg to the pan, mix, and serve hot.

Takoyaki (Octopus Balls)

Ingredients:

- 1 cup flour
- 1 cup dashi or water
- 1 egg
- ½ cup chopped octopus
- ¼ cup green onions, chopped
- ¼ cup tempura scraps (tenkasu)
- Takoyaki sauce
- Mayonnaise
- Bonito flakes

Instructions:

1. Mix flour, dashi, and egg into a smooth batter.
2. Heat a takoyaki pan and grease lightly.
3. Pour batter into the molds and add octopus, green onions, and tempura scraps.
4. Cook, turning frequently, until golden brown.
5. Drizzle with takoyaki sauce, mayonnaise, and bonito flakes. Serve hot.

Tempura (Battered & Fried Seafood/Veggies)

Ingredients:

- ½ lb shrimp or mixed vegetables (sweet potato, zucchini, eggplant)
- 1 cup flour
- 1 cup ice-cold water
- 1 egg
- Oil for frying
- Tempura dipping sauce

Instructions:

1. In a bowl, mix cold water and egg. Add flour and mix lightly (don't overmix).
2. Heat oil to 350°F (175°C).
3. Dip shrimp/vegetables in the batter and fry until crispy.
4. Drain and serve with tempura dipping sauce.

Shoyu (Soy Sauce) Ramen

Ingredients:

- 4 cups chicken broth
- 2 tbsp soy sauce
- 1 tbsp mirin
- ½ tsp sesame oil
- 1 garlic clove, minced
- 2 packs fresh or dried ramen noodles
- ½ cup bamboo shoots
- 2 boiled eggs, halved
- Green onions and nori for garnish

Instructions:

1. Heat sesame oil in a pot, add garlic, and sauté until fragrant.
2. Add broth, soy sauce, and mirin, and bring to a simmer.
3. Cook noodles according to package instructions and drain.
4. Divide noodles into bowls, pour hot broth over them, and top with bamboo shoots, boiled eggs, green onions, and nori.

Oyakodon (Chicken and Egg Rice Bowl)

Ingredients:

- 1 chicken thigh, sliced
- ½ onion, sliced
- 1 cup dashi
- 2 tbsp soy sauce
- 1 tbsp mirin
- 1 egg, beaten
- 1 cup cooked rice
- Green onions for garnish

Instructions:

1. In a pan, heat dashi, soy sauce, and mirin. Add onion and cook until soft.
2. Add chicken and simmer until cooked through.
3. Pour beaten egg over and let it set for 1-2 minutes.
4. Serve over rice, garnished with green onions.

Yaki Onigiri (Grilled Rice Balls)

Ingredients:

- 2 cups cooked rice
- 1 tbsp soy sauce
- 1 tbsp miso paste (optional)
- 1 tsp sesame oil
- Nori for wrapping (optional)

Instructions:

1. Wet hands and shape rice into balls or triangles.
2. Mix soy sauce and miso paste, then brush onto rice balls.
3. Heat a pan or grill and cook rice balls until crispy and golden.
4. Wrap with nori and serve.

Sukiyaki (Beef Hot Pot)

Ingredients:

- ½ lb thinly sliced beef
- 4 cups dashi or water
- ¼ cup soy sauce
- 2 tbsp mirin
- 1 tbsp sugar
- ½ block tofu, cut into cubes
- 1 cup Napa cabbage, chopped
- ½ cup mushrooms (shiitake or enoki)
- ½ cup sliced onion
- ½ cup sliced carrots
- 2 green onions, chopped
- 1 pack udon noodles (optional)

Instructions:

1. In a pot, mix dashi, soy sauce, mirin, and sugar. Bring to a simmer.
2. Add vegetables, tofu, and mushrooms. Simmer for 5 minutes.
3. Add sliced beef and cook briefly until no longer pink.
4. Serve hot with rice or udon noodles.

Nabe (Japanese Hot Pot)

Ingredients:

- 4 cups dashi broth
- ½ lb thinly sliced chicken or seafood
- ½ block tofu, cubed
- 1 cup Napa cabbage, chopped
- ½ cup mushrooms (shiitake or enoki)
- ½ cup sliced carrots
- 1 green onion, sliced
- 1 pack udon noodles (optional)
- Ponzu sauce for dipping

Instructions:

1. In a large pot, bring dashi broth to a boil.
2. Add vegetables, tofu, and mushrooms, simmering for 5 minutes.
3. Add chicken or seafood and cook until done.
4. Serve with ponzu sauce for dipping.

Omurice (Omelette Rice)

Ingredients:

- 2 cups cooked rice
- ½ cup cooked chicken, diced
- ½ cup mixed vegetables (peas, carrots, corn)
- 2 tbsp ketchup
- 1 tbsp soy sauce
- 2 eggs
- 1 tbsp butter
- Salt and pepper to taste

Instructions:

1. Heat butter in a pan and sauté chicken and vegetables.
2. Add rice, soy sauce, and ketchup. Stir-fry until well mixed.
3. In another pan, cook a thin omelette.
4. Place rice mixture in the center of the omelette and fold over.
5. Serve with extra ketchup on top.

Chawanmushi (Savory Egg Custard)

Ingredients:

- 2 eggs
- 1 cup dashi broth
- 1 tsp soy sauce
- ½ tsp mirin
- 2 shrimp, peeled
- ½ block tofu, cubed
- 2 mushrooms, sliced

Instructions:

1. Beat eggs and mix with dashi, soy sauce, and mirin. Strain the mixture.
2. Divide tofu, shrimp, and mushrooms into small cups.
3. Pour the egg mixture over the ingredients.
4. Steam for 15 minutes until set. Serve warm.

Japanese Potato Salad

Ingredients:

- 3 medium potatoes, boiled and mashed
- ½ cup cucumber, thinly sliced
- ½ cup carrots, finely chopped
- ¼ cup onion, finely chopped
- ½ cup mayonnaise
- 1 tsp rice vinegar
- Salt and pepper to taste

Instructions:

1. Boil potatoes until tender, mash, and let cool.
2. Mix with cucumber, carrots, and onion.
3. Stir in mayonnaise, rice vinegar, salt, and pepper.
4. Chill before serving.

Salmon Teriyaki

Ingredients:

- 2 salmon fillets
- 2 tbsp soy sauce
- 1 tbsp mirin
- 1 tbsp sugar
- 1 tbsp sake (optional)
- 1 tsp sesame oil

Instructions:

1. Mix soy sauce, mirin, sugar, and sake. Marinate salmon for 10 minutes.
2. Heat sesame oil in a pan and cook salmon for 3 minutes per side.
3. Pour marinade into the pan and cook until thickened.
4. Serve hot with rice.

Shabu-Shabu (Japanese Hot Pot)

Ingredients:

- 4 cups dashi broth
- ½ lb thinly sliced beef or pork
- ½ block tofu, cubed
- 1 cup Napa cabbage, chopped
- ½ cup mushrooms (shiitake or enoki)
- ½ cup sliced carrots
- 1 green onion, sliced
- Ponzu or sesame dipping sauce

Instructions:

1. Bring dashi broth to a boil in a large pot.
2. Add vegetables and tofu, cooking for 5 minutes.
3. Dip meat slices in the hot broth until cooked.
4. Serve with ponzu or sesame sauce.

Agedashi Tofu (Fried Tofu in Dashi)

Ingredients:

- 1 block firm tofu, cut into cubes
- ¼ cup cornstarch
- Oil for frying
- ½ cup dashi broth
- 1 tbsp soy sauce
- 1 tbsp mirin
- Green onions for garnish

Instructions:

1. Coat tofu cubes in cornstarch.
2. Heat oil and fry tofu until golden.
3. In a pot, heat dashi, soy sauce, and mirin.
4. Pour broth over fried tofu and garnish with green onions.

Hiyayakko (Chilled Tofu)

Ingredients:

- 1 block silken tofu
- 2 tbsp soy sauce
- 1 green onion, sliced
- 1 tsp grated ginger
- 1 tbsp bonito flakes (optional)

Instructions:

1. Cut tofu into cubes and place in a bowl.
2. Top with green onions, ginger, and bonito flakes.
3. Drizzle with soy sauce and serve chilled.

Mentaiko Pasta (Spicy Cod Roe Pasta)

Ingredients:

- 2 servings spaghetti
- 2 tbsp butter
- 2 tbsp mentaiko (spicy cod roe)
- 1 tbsp soy sauce
- 2 tbsp heavy cream (optional)
- 1 green onion, sliced
- Nori for garnish

Instructions:

1. Cook spaghetti according to package instructions and drain.
2. Melt butter in a pan, then mix in mentaiko, soy sauce, and cream.
3. Toss spaghetti in the sauce.
4. Garnish with green onions and nori. Serve hot.

Unagi Don (Grilled Eel Rice Bowl)

Ingredients:

- 1 fillet grilled unagi (Japanese eel)
- 2 cups cooked Japanese rice
- 2 tbsp unagi sauce (store-bought or homemade)
- 1 tsp sesame seeds (optional)
- ½ sheet nori, sliced into thin strips
- 1 green onion, sliced

Instructions:

1. Heat the unagi in a pan or oven at 350°F (175°C) for 5 minutes.
2. Brush unagi sauce over the eel and heat for another 2 minutes.
3. Place cooked rice in a bowl and top with the grilled eel.
4. Drizzle with more unagi sauce, then garnish with sesame seeds, nori, and green onion.

Yasai Itame (Stir-Fried Vegetables)

Ingredients:

- 1 cup cabbage, sliced
- ½ cup carrots, julienned
- ½ cup bell peppers, sliced
- ½ cup bean sprouts
- 1 tbsp soy sauce
- 1 tbsp oyster sauce
- 1 tbsp sesame oil
- 1 clove garlic, minced

Instructions:

1. Heat sesame oil in a pan and sauté garlic.
2. Add cabbage, carrots, and bell peppers. Stir-fry for 3 minutes.
3. Add bean sprouts, soy sauce, and oyster sauce. Stir well and cook for another 2 minutes.
4. Serve hot as a side dish.

Japanese Hamburg Steak

Ingredients:

- ½ lb ground beef
- ½ lb ground pork
- ½ small onion, finely chopped
- ½ cup panko breadcrumbs
- 1 egg
- 2 tbsp milk
- ½ tsp salt
- ¼ tsp black pepper
- 1 tbsp oil
- 3 tbsp Worcestershire sauce
- 2 tbsp ketchup

Instructions:

1. Mix ground meat, onion, breadcrumbs, egg, milk, salt, and pepper in a bowl.
2. Shape into patties.
3. Heat oil in a pan and cook patties for 4 minutes per side.
4. Mix Worcestershire sauce and ketchup, then pour over patties. Simmer for 2 minutes.

Simmered Daikon Radish

Ingredients:

- 1 daikon radish, peeled and sliced into thick rounds
- 3 cups dashi broth
- 2 tbsp soy sauce
- 1 tbsp mirin
- 1 tbsp sugar
- ½ tsp salt

Instructions:

1. In a pot, bring dashi broth to a boil.
2. Add daikon slices and simmer for 20 minutes.
3. Add soy sauce, mirin, sugar, and salt. Simmer for another 10 minutes.
4. Serve warm with broth.

Corn Potage (Japanese Corn Soup)

Ingredients:

- 1½ cups corn kernels
- 1½ cups milk
- ½ cup heavy cream
- 1 small onion, chopped
- 1 tbsp butter
- Salt and pepper to taste

Instructions:

1. Heat butter in a pot and sauté onions until soft.
2. Add corn and cook for 2 minutes.
3. Blend with milk until smooth.
4. Return to the pot, add heavy cream, and heat gently. Season with salt and pepper.

Karaage (Japanese Fried Chicken)

Ingredients:

- ½ lb boneless chicken thighs, cut into bite-sized pieces
- 2 tbsp soy sauce
- 1 tbsp sake
- 1 clove garlic, grated
- 1 tsp ginger, grated
- ½ cup potato starch (or cornstarch)
- Oil for frying

Instructions:

1. Marinate chicken in soy sauce, sake, garlic, and ginger for 30 minutes.
2. Coat with potato starch.
3. Heat oil and fry chicken for 3-4 minutes until golden brown.
4. Drain on paper towels and serve hot.

Tsukemono (Japanese Pickles)

Ingredients:

- 1 cucumber, thinly sliced
- ½ tsp salt
- 1 tbsp rice vinegar
- ½ tsp sugar
- 1 tsp sesame seeds

Instructions:

1. Sprinkle salt over cucumbers and let sit for 10 minutes.
2. Rinse and drain.
3. Mix with rice vinegar, sugar, and sesame seeds.
4. Let sit for 30 minutes before serving.

Chashu Pork (Braised Pork for Ramen)

Ingredients:

- ½ lb pork belly
- 2 cups water
- ¼ cup soy sauce
- 2 tbsp sake
- 1 tbsp sugar
- 1 clove garlic, smashed
- 1-inch piece ginger, sliced

Instructions:

1. Sear pork belly on all sides in a hot pan.
2. Add water, soy sauce, sake, sugar, garlic, and ginger.
3. Simmer for 1 hour, turning occasionally.
4. Slice and serve over ramen or rice.

Lotus Root Stir-Fry

Ingredients:

- 1 lotus root, peeled and sliced
- 1 tbsp soy sauce
- 1 tbsp mirin
- 1 tsp sugar
- 1 tsp sesame oil
- 1 tsp sesame seeds

Instructions:

1. Blanch lotus root slices in boiling water for 2 minutes.
2. Heat sesame oil in a pan and stir-fry lotus root.
3. Add soy sauce, mirin, and sugar. Stir-fry for 2 minutes.
4. Sprinkle with sesame seeds before serving.

Japanese Cabbage Pancakes (Okonomiyaki Style)

Ingredients:

- 2 cups shredded cabbage
- ½ cup flour
- ½ cup dashi broth or water
- 1 egg
- ¼ tsp salt
- 1 tbsp oil
- Okonomiyaki sauce, mayonnaise, and bonito flakes for topping

Instructions:

1. Mix cabbage, flour, dashi, egg, and salt in a bowl.
2. Heat oil in a pan and spread the batter into a round pancake.
3. Cook for 3-4 minutes per side until golden brown.
4. Top with okonomiyaki sauce, mayonnaise, and bonito flakes.

Gomaae (Sesame Spinach Salad)

Ingredients:

- 1 bunch spinach
- 2 tbsp sesame seeds, toasted
- 1 tbsp soy sauce
- 1 tsp sugar
- 1 tsp mirin

Instructions:

1. Blanch spinach in boiling water for 30 seconds, then drain and cool in ice water.
2. Squeeze excess water and cut into bite-sized pieces.
3. Grind toasted sesame seeds, then mix with soy sauce, sugar, and mirin.
4. Toss the spinach in the sesame dressing and serve.

Mitarashi Dango (Sweet Soy Sauce Glazed Dumplings)

Ingredients:

- 1 cup glutinous rice flour (shiratamako)
- ½ cup water
- 2 tbsp soy sauce
- 2 tbsp sugar
- 1 tbsp mirin
- ½ tbsp cornstarch mixed with 1 tbsp water

Instructions:

1. Mix rice flour with water to form a dough.
2. Roll into small balls and boil until they float. Drain and cool.
3. Skewer 3-4 dumplings onto sticks.
4. In a pan, heat soy sauce, sugar, and mirin, then add cornstarch mixture to thicken.
5. Brush glaze over dumplings and serve.

Kinpira Gobo (Braised Burdock Root)

Ingredients:

- 1 burdock root, julienned
- ½ carrot, julienned
- 1 tbsp soy sauce
- 1 tbsp mirin
- 1 tsp sugar
- 1 tsp sesame oil
- ½ tsp sesame seeds

Instructions:

1. Soak burdock root in water for 10 minutes, then drain.
2. Heat sesame oil in a pan and stir-fry burdock and carrot.
3. Add soy sauce, mirin, and sugar. Cook for 3-4 minutes.
4. Sprinkle with sesame seeds before serving.

Miso Glazed Eggplant

Ingredients:

- 1 large eggplant, sliced in half
- 2 tbsp miso paste
- 1 tbsp mirin
- 1 tbsp sugar
- 1 tbsp sake
- 1 tsp sesame oil

Instructions:

1. Brush eggplant with sesame oil and grill for 5 minutes.
2. Mix miso, mirin, sugar, and sake, then spread over eggplant.
3. Broil for another 2-3 minutes until caramelized.
4. Serve warm with sesame seeds on top.

Kinpira Renkon (Stir-Fried Lotus Root)

Ingredients:

- 1 lotus root, peeled and sliced
- 1 tbsp soy sauce
- 1 tbsp mirin
- 1 tsp sugar
- 1 tsp sesame oil
- 1 tsp sesame seeds

Instructions:

1. Blanch lotus root slices in boiling water for 2 minutes.
2. Heat sesame oil in a pan and stir-fry lotus root.
3. Add soy sauce, mirin, and sugar. Stir-fry for 2 minutes.
4. Sprinkle with sesame seeds before serving.

Dorayaki (Sweet Red Bean Pancakes)

Ingredients:

- 1 cup flour
- 2 tbsp sugar
- 1 tsp baking powder
- 1 egg
- ½ cup milk
- 1 tbsp honey
- ½ cup sweet red bean paste (anko)

Instructions:

1. Mix flour, sugar, and baking powder. Add egg, milk, and honey. Stir until smooth.
2. Heat a pan and pour batter to form small pancakes. Cook until bubbles form, then flip.
3. Let pancakes cool, then sandwich red bean paste between two pancakes.

Matcha Warabi Mochi

Ingredients:

- ½ cup warabi starch (bracken starch)
- 1½ cups water
- ¼ cup sugar
- 1 tbsp matcha powder
- ¼ cup kinako (roasted soybean flour)
- 1 tbsp honey (optional)

Instructions:

1. Mix warabi starch, water, sugar, and matcha powder in a pot.
2. Heat over low, stirring constantly, until thick and translucent.
3. Pour into a mold and chill for 1 hour.
4. Cut into cubes and coat with kinako. Drizzle with honey if desired.

Castella Cake (Japanese Sponge Cake)

Ingredients:

- 4 eggs
- ½ cup sugar
- ½ cup honey
- 1 cup bread flour
- 2 tbsp warm milk

Instructions:

1. Beat eggs and sugar until pale and thick.
2. Add honey and milk, then gradually fold in flour.
3. Pour into a lined baking pan and bake at 320°F (160°C) for 40 minutes.
4. Let cool, then slice and serve.

Daifuku Mochi (Sweet Rice Cake with Filling)

Ingredients:

- 1 cup glutinous rice flour
- ½ cup water
- ¼ cup sugar
- ½ cup sweet red bean paste (anko)
- Potato starch for dusting

Instructions:

1. Mix rice flour, water, and sugar. Microwave for 1 minute, stir, then microwave for another minute until dough is sticky.
2. Dust a surface with potato starch and roll out mochi dough.
3. Place a spoonful of red bean paste in the center and fold mochi around it.
4. Shape into balls and serve.

www.ingramcontent.com/pod-product-compliance
Lightning Source LLC
LaVergne TN
LVHW081340060526
838201LV00055B/2759

9798348103996